W0410528

Astrid Berger • Gabriele Broniowski

Aufsteigen ... Englisch 4 Schularbeiten

So schaffst du die **4. Klasse**
HS/AHS
und Neue Mittelschule

G&G

TEST 1

I FOCUS ON GRAMMAR

1. Use comparisons to complete the text

You write about your summer holidays which were not as nice as you had hoped they would be.

It took us ________________ (long) to get to Venice ____________ last year. The rooms were ________________ (dirty) this year ________________ last year. The food was not ________________ (good) ________________ we had thought it would be. The restaurants were ______________________ (crowded) and ______________________ (expensive) there ____________ in Austria. The weather was ________________ (bad) ____________ in Salzburg. There were ________________ (many) other tourists ________________ we had expected. The people were not ________________ (friendly) ________________ we had expected.

2. Use active or passive forms (past tense) to complete the text

The Aborigines

The first Aborigines ______________________ (come) to Australia about 40,000 years ago. They ______________________ (live) in small family groups. Since 1788 British settlers ______________________ (take) away the Aborigines' land. When white men wanted the Aborigines' land, they simply ______________________ (drive) them off.

Aborigines ______________________ (often hunt) and killed by the white men, and children of mixed race ______________________ (take) away and were given to white families as servants. They ______________________ (tell) to forget their language and their culture. Then they ______________________ (teach) English.

From the 1970s on, a lot of money ______________________ (spend) to give the Aborigines a better education and better health care. Some of their land __________________________ (give) back.

In 2008 the Australian government _____________________________ (apologise) for the way Aborigines ______________________ (treat) in the past.

3. Use some/any + compounds (e.g. somewhere, anywhere, somebody ...)

1. Oh no, where is my English homework now? I cannot find it ______________________, but I finished it only _____________ minutes ago! It must be ______________________ on the desk, I haven't put it ______________________ else and I haven't shown it to ______________________ . Ah, ______________________ must have taken it.

I guess it was my darling twin sister, Lisa.

2. "Lisa, have you taken ______________________ of my DVDs?!" –

"Yes, I borrowed ______________________ of your DVDs, but I put them back again."

"Oh dear, you always take anything you like and then you just put it ________________ where I can't find it. I hate that!" – "Oh come on, would you like to watch ________________ of my DVDs? There isn't ________________ reason to be mad at me!"

II READING COMPREHENSION

Western Australia is the largest state in the world and covers one-third of the Australian continent. It is famous for its brilliant blue skies, warm sunny climate and white sandy beaches. 850 km north of Perth in Western Australia, there is an attraction that all Australians and visitors should see and experience - the Dolphins of Monkey Mia. There have now been three generations of these intelligent creatures that probably look at people and wonder what they are up to. They have been visiting the area for over 30 years now and the current group of dolphins that frequent the bay area numbers around 100. It's an unforgettable experience when these wonderful animals are fed by the rangers.

There is a separate beach area, which is strictly controlled, that allows people to swim with the dolphins and watch them up close. You definitely get the feeling that the dolphins are doing the same. They come into the beach most mornings between 7 am and midday and visitors can walk amongst the dolphins in the shallow waters.

Monkey Mia beach is part of the Shark Bay World Heritage region of Western Australia, where about 400 dolphins but also over 10,000 dugongs have their home. The dugong is one of the two surviving species of sea cows left in the world.

The Northern Territory is the third largest Australian territory and it is home to Australia's largest population of Aboriginal people. Although it covers a large area it is sparsely populated. Darwin is the capital of the Northern Territory. It has a relaxed outdoor lifestyle and offers warm weather all around the year.

Three hours east of Darwin you find the famous Kakadu National Park. It is Australia's largest national park, with one thousand species of flora (plants), 30 mammals, 75 reptiles, 1,500 butterflies and moths, 50 freshwater fish and 25 species of frog.

Over thousands of years, Aboriginal people have left behind extraordinary Aboriginal art, with rock sites dating back 25,000 years. More than 1,000 sites have been found.

The Kata Tjuta National Park is 280 miles (450 km) southwest of Alice Springs, the capital of the Outback, which is situated right in the centre of Australia. Ayers Rock or Uluru, the world's largest monolith and an Aboriginal sacred site, is Australia's most famous natural landmark. Visitors can climb to the top or take a walking tour around the rock with an Aboriginal guide.

Tick (✓) the correct answer

1. Darwin is the capital of

A		Western Australia.
B		Victoria.
C		The Northern Territory.
D		Queensland.

2. Monkey Mia is the home of hundreds of

A		monkeys.
B		frogs.
C		sharks.
D		dolphins.

3. The dugong is a

A		dolphin.
B		sea cow.
C		shark.
D		seal.

4. Three hours east of Darwin you find the famous

A		Kata Tjuta National Park.
B		Olgas.
C		Kakadu National Park.
D		Ayers Rock.

5. Kakadu National Park is famous for its

A		plants, animals, Aboriginal art.
B		flora, mammals, birds.
C		frogs, corals, plants.
D		reptiles, butterflies, dolphins.

6. The capital of the Outback is

A		Sydney.
B		Perth.
C		Darwin.
D		Alice Springs.

III WRITING TASK

As you are interested in pen friends from all over the world you became a member of the International Friendship Club about a month ago.

Last week you got the name and e-mail address of a 14-year-old boy/girl in Australia.

Write the first e-mail to this boy/girl. Your mail should be about 150 words.

In your e-mail you must:

- describe what you look like
- give information about your family
- tell him/her about your interests/hobbies
- tell him/her what you do in your free time
- give information about Austria and the town you live in
- ask him/her questions you want him/her to answer in his/her reply

TEST 2

I FOCUS ON GRAMMAR

1. Comparison: Use (not) as ... as/than where necessary and the appropriate (= geeignete) form of the adjective

Many health experts say that we should eat ________________ (much/mehr) vegetables and ________________ (little/weniger) meat. They also say that fast food is ________________ ________________ (not dangerous) ________________ junk food because fast food can also be an apple, some yoghurt or a piece of cheese.

Young people buy junk food because it is often ________________ (cheap) ________________ healthy food.

Cooking is ________________ (easy) ________________ in the past because there is a wide range of frozen or canned food to choose from. But although there is enough food, people are ________________ (not healthy) ________________ they could be because they eat the wrong things.

Becoming a vegetarian is ________________ (popular) ________________ in the past, especially for teenagers.

2. Use active or passive forms (past) to complete the text

Long ago, the first Navajos ________________ (live) in northwestern Canada and Alaska. Over 1,000 years ago they ________________ (begin) to travel south and ________________ (reach) the southwestern United States. They ________________ (meet) farmers who are known as Pueblo Indians, and the Navajo ________________ (settle) near them and ________________ (learn) from them. The Navajo ________________ (teach) them how to plant corn, beans, squash and melon. The homes of the Navajo Indians ________________ (call) hogans. They ________________ (make) from wooden poles, tree bark and mud.

After the Spanish settled in the 1600's, the Navajo began to steal sheep and horses from them. The Navajo ________________ (start) to use the animals in their daily life. The wool ________________ (use) to make clothes, blankets and rugs. The meat ________________ (use) for food.

They used the horses to travel longer distances and also used them to begin trading.

Pottery, blankets and rugs ________________ (take) to towns to be sold there.

Then trading posts ________________ (build) on reservations, so handmade crafts, such as pottery and blankets ________________ (can sell) there.

3. Complete the if-clauses

1. Tom is reading the newspaper. There is a lot about economic problems, war and violence. Tom is getting angry. He thinks, "If I ________________ (be) an important politician,

I ________________ (try) to help people."

2. Walking through town you notice a poster announcing a concert of your favourite pop-star. You say "If there ________________ (be) still tickets available, I ________________ (buy) tickets."

3. Looking out of the window in the morning you are surprised by the nice weather. You say, "If the weather ________________ (be) like that in the afternoon, I ________________ (go) for a walk."

4. Your friend asks you to take him to the airport. Unfortunately your car has broken down. You say, "I'm so sorry! If I ________________ (have) a car, I ________________ (take) you to the airport."

II READING COMPREHENSION

Extreme sports are developed for everybody, not just crazy kids who want to test their limits. Now New Zealand once again leads the world in stupid things to do.

You may have tried bungee jumping, sky diving, white water rafting or other fun activities to feel energised but if you are willing to try something radical, completely different from other adventure sports, then you've got to try Sphereing®! You get the chance to take part in a totally bizarre and fun experience. You are protected by a massive cushion of air while screaming your lungs out.

Sphereing®, also called zorbing™ or globe-riding, is the latest trend sport. People roll down a hill in a sphere, generally made of transparent plastic. Sphereing is usually done on a gentle slope, but can also be done on a level surface or on water. There the rider has more control. Where there are no hills available people have begun constructing metal ramps.

Most spheres are constructed for a single rider, but some hold two or three. The longer runs are approximately half a mile. Globe-riding is very popular in New Zealand and the very first Zorb site was in Rotorua.

The sphere is a double-hulled sphere, with one ball inside the other with an air layer in between. This acts as a shock absorber for the rider.

Many spheres have straps to hold the rider in place, others leave the rider free to walk the sphere around or be tossed about freely by the rolling motion. A typical sphere is about 3 metres in diameter, with an inner sphere size of about 2 metres, leaving a 50 – 60 centimetre air cushion around the riders. Spheres usually have one or two tunnel-like entrances.

Mark the following statements true (T) or false (F)

	T	F
1. Spheres can only be used by one person at a time.		
2. Globe-riding is very popular in Australia.		
3. Spheres are usually made of transparent plastic.		
4. Longer runs are usually half a mile.		
5. Globe-riding can be done on water too.		
6. A sphere must at least be 4 metres in diameter.		
7. Inside a sphere you are well protected.		

III WRITING TASK

You have an e-mail friend in the USA. At school he/she is doing a project about sports all over the world. He/She has asked you for information about sports in Austria and how teenagers feel about sports.

In your e-mail you must:

- tell him/her what sports you practice and/or are interested in
- explain which sports are popular with teenagers in Austria
- describe what kind of sports are offered at your school
- give some information about your family and sports

Your e-mail should be about 150 words.

TEST 3

I FOCUS ON GRAMMAR

1. Restate the following negative statements twice, using comparative adjectives

e.g. February isn't as long as March (short/long)

a. February is shorter than March.

b. March is longer than February.

1. Peter doesn't eat as much junk food as John (little/much).
2. Learning Chinese isn't as easy as learning English (easy/difficult).
3. In February the weather isn't as good as in June or July (bad/good).
4. Reality TV shows aren't as interesting as action movies (interesting/boring).

2. Use some/any + compounds (e.g. something, somewhere, anywhere, somebody ...)

1. Yesterday mum and I went shopping. I saw ________________ nice T-shirts but I did not buy __________________ because mum said they were too expensive.
2. I would like ________________________ to drink. Is there _______________ orange juice left?
3. If you believe in yourself and work hard you can achieve (= erreichen) almost _______________. Well, ________________ people are just lucky and are born rich.
4. Is there ________________________ I can do to help you? You look tired and exhausted. – Well, in fact there is ________________________ you can do for me. We need _______________ milk and I am too tired to go out again.
5. Did ________________________ call while I was out? Yes, a boy called Bob rang and wanted to know if your English teacher had given you ______________________ handouts last Monday.
6. In my last summer holidays I did not go _____________________. I had to study for my exam in autumn and did not have time for a summer job. Therefore I did not have ________________________ money. I did not even go on _______________ daytrips.

3. Use reported speech to change the dialogue into a text

Yesterday Tim had a test. After the test he and his mum talked about it:

- Mrs Johnson: How was your English test? (She asked ...)
- Tim: We had to make up an interview with Morgan Spurlock. He is the guy who only ate Mc Donald's food for a month. It was an experiment. (He answered ... He added ...)
- Mrs Johnson: Did Morgan like eating all that junk food? (She wanted to know ...)
- Tim: I don't really know. After 22 days his doctors told him to stop the experiment but he didn't listen to them. (He replied ...)
- Mrs Johnson: I hope Morgan didn't have any serious problems. (She said ...)

II READING COMPREHENSION

The dangers of fast food

Every day, about one-quarter of American adults eat at a fast-food restaurant. Fast food is cheap, tasty and can be prepared quickly. Unfortunately fast food is high in saturated fat and calories, but it is low in fibre and nutrients. As a result half of America's adults and one-quarter of its children are obese (fettsüchtig), double the rate of a generation ago. Some people think chicken nuggets are a healthier alternative, but even they are flavoured with beef extract and contain twice as much fat as an ordinary hamburger.

Although most people do not have health problems related to fast food until they are in their forties – obesity and diabetes are at the top of the list – the problems already start before children enter kindergarten. Children can be influenced quite easily and therefore fast-food chains target children in their advertising campaigns. About 96% of American school-aged children recognize Ronald McDonald, almost every American child eats at a fast food restaurant at least once a month.

Fast food uses cheap labour, usually supplied by teenagers. Although a part-time job can teach teenagers responsibility, teenage boys who work long hours are more likely to use drugs and get into trouble.

Working in a fast food restaurant can also be dangerous. Each year about 20,000 teenagers are injured, about twice as many as adults.

To keep meat prices low, most slaughterhouses (Schlachthäuser) have moved out of big cities and into small towns. Some people claim that instead of hiring skilled workers, meatpacking plants often employ immigrants who are willing to work hard for little money on assembly lines that turn living cattle into frozen hamburgers at record speed. Each year, at least one-third of all meatpackers are injured on the job.

To counteract the dangers of fast food and fast life the organization Slow Food was founded in 1989. Its members want to make sure that local food traditions do not disappear and they want people to know more about the food they eat, where it comes from, how it tastes and how our food choices affect the rest of the world.

They say "Slow Food" is good, clean and fair food. The organization believes that the food we eat should taste good, that it should be produced in a clean way that does not harm the environment, the animals or our health, and that food producers should receive fair compensation for their work.

Mark the following statements true (T) or false (F)

	T	F
1. Every day about one third of American adults eat at a fast food restaurant.		
2. Fast food is high in fat, fibre and nutrients.		
3. Chicken nuggets are healthier because they contain less fat than hamburgers.		
4. Most people do not have health problems until middle age.		
5. Fast food chains employ teenagers because they are often cheaper than adults.		

6. More teenagers than adults are injured while working in a fast food place.		
7. Slaughterhouses have moved out of big cities and to small towns.		
8. The organization Slow Food was founded to help people who work for fast food chains.		
9. Slow Food wants people to be more interested in the food they eat.		
10. Slow Food believes that food producers should get a fair price for their products.		

III WRITING TASK

You have an e-mail friend in the USA. At school he/she is doing a project on food and eating habits all over the world. He/She has asked you for information about food in Austria.

In your e-mail you must include information

- about the kind of food you like and what your eating habits are
- about your national cuisine (traditional Austrian food)
- about the kind of food teenagers and people your age prefer and why
- what you think about fast food, junk food or healthy food

Your e-mail should be about 150–180 words.

TEST 4

I FOCUS ON GRAMMAR

1. Make passive sentences

1. Tim/ask/to leave the room/yesterday.
2. This newspaper/read/many people/every day.
3. The supermarket around the corner/close/next week.
4. You/ever/attack/dog?
5. A new government/elect/next Sunday.
6. Many Sioux/kill/at Wounded Knee/in 1890.

2. Fill in the correct tenses

1. Sarah told us that she ________________ (see) our teacher at the cinema the day before.
2. If I ________________ (not miss) the train I will be on time.
3. Paul said that he ________________ (never talk) to me again.
4. George isn't very good at playing squash because he ____________________ (not play) for a very long time.

3. Fill in adjective or adverb

1. You must go and see the show. It's ________________ (absolute) terrific.
2. Paul speaks Russian ________________ (fluent).
3. This is such an ________________ (interesting) book. It has ________________ (complete) changed my opinion on modern art.
4. You look so ________________ (good) in this dress.
You should always wear ________________ (colourful) clothes.
5. Sam has been absent for a week now. I hope he is not ________________ (serious) ill.
6. Don't give up so ____________ (quick)! You have worked so ________________ (hard), I'm sure you will pass the exam!
7. Let's go to the cinema! – Yeah, sounds ________________ (good).

II READING COMPREHENSION

Native Americans today

Today there are about two million Native Americans in the United States and one million in Canada. The term "Native American" includes over 500 different groups. Not all of them live in similar situations. There are those who live in reservations but between one-third and one-half of the Indian population in the United States now lives in cities. On the whole Native

Americans living in cities are better off than those spending their lives in reservations. But they are still among the poorest people. In 2004 21% of Native American families lived below the federal poverty line (Armutsgrenze).
The main problems all Native American communities have to cope with are unemployment, high school drop out rates, alcoholism, high crime rates, health problems and discrimination. Some years ago statistics said that three of the ten poorest counties in the USA were Sioux reservations in South Dakota.
Today Native Americans are looking for ways to improve their difficult social and economic situation. One idea has proved quite successful. Some tribes founded casinos on Indian reservations. This meant jobs for a lot of people. The profit they made helped to build schools, improve the infrastructure and to preserve Native American traditions. Today there are about 400 Indian casinos in the United States.
There are many Native American languages but most children no longer learn the language of their fathers and so these languages may die out. Today there are already many Native Americans who have grown up without their native language, and it is difficult to learn a new language as an adult. Therefore some communities are trying to find older people who teach the youngest generation the language before it is too late.
Native American art, on the other hand, has become very popular over the years. Many Indian artists sell their products to both tourists and serious art collectors.

Mark the following statements true (T) or false (F)

	T	F
1. Most Native Americans live in cities.		
2. The situation in the reservations is better than in the cities.		
3. Many Native Americans are alcoholics.		
4. There are no Sioux in North Dakota.		
5. Lots of Native Americans lost their jobs because of the casinos.		
6. It is easier to learn a language when you are still a kid.		
7. Nobody wants to buy Native American art.		

III WRITING TASK

Write a story using the following beginning

When Paul woke up in the morning and looked out of his tent he was confused. The ground in front of his tent was full of footprints that had not been there the night before. Nobody had been there last night, nobody but Paul. He was on a hiking trip in Canyonland National Park in Utah, USA. He had decided to do this trip all on his own because he wanted to get away from the stress of the big city and enjoy the solitude (Einsamkeit) of nature. But now he felt uneasy. He examined the footprints and suddenly saw a knife lying on the ground. Paul wanted to pick it up, when ...

Your story should be 150–180 words.

120–150

TEST 5

I FOCUS ON GRAMMAR

1. Fill in "will" or "going to"

1. I think Tom ______________________ (probably be) here in the afternoon.
2. I've got to go now. Perhaps I _________________ (see) you later.
3. Are you free tomorrow night? – Sorry, I ______________________ (have) dinner with my cousin and his wife.
4. Paul has plans for his future. He ______________________ (study) engineering.
5. I hope we _________________ (get) tickets for the show.

2. Fill in the correct forms: adjective or adverb

When Jane came home she was _________________ (tired). It had been a _________________ (long) day at the office. When she passed the mirror she noticed that she looked _________________ (terrible). "Nobody home?" Jane shouted _________________ (loud). No answer. "Where is everybody?" she thought _________________ (angry). She had worked so _________________ (hard) all day and had been looking forward to a _________________ (nice) evening with her husband and the children. Sam had promised to make dinner. Now, nobody was at home.
_________________ (quick) Jane took her handbag and left the flat again. "Well, then I'll have dinner at my favourite restaurant "Luigi's" round the corner. Sam's spaghetti don't taste _________________ (good) anyway," she thought. When she opened the door of the restaurant the waiter greeted her _______________ (friendly) way. "Your husband and the children are already waiting for you," he said. And now Jane remembered: Sam had said that tonight they were going to have dinner at "Luigi's"!

3. Rewrite the text using reported speech

Peter's dad promised, "You will get a new computer game if you pass the exam." "I haven't got enough time to study for the exam," Peter answered. "You work all day and I have to look after Cathie when you and mum are not at home. Everything was easier when mum was at home. But now she has a job. So it's always me who must do everything!" Peter complained. "Things will be better next month. Then I'll be able to work from home," Peter's mother said.

II READING COMPREHENSION

Paintball

Sometimes you read that paintball is one of the fastest growing extreme sports. It is played by a steadily growing number of people all over the world. Still, there is the question whether we can really call paintball an extreme sport because it is neither extremely dangerous nor do you need special athletic skills to play it. Team spirit and tactical intelligence are more important. Paintball was invented about twenty years ago in the USA. The aim of paintball is for one team to eliminate all the members of the other team using a special gun and "bullets" filled with paint. When you are hit the game is over for you. That is why some players get very angry when they get hit. Their team can go on playing but they can only watch.

People who play paintball say that it is a good way to get away from all the stress of everyday life. For playing paintball you don't have to buy expensive equipment. Usually you can rent a paintball gun and protective clothing at your local paintball field. It is a very safe sport. Everybody can play paintball as long as they are over ten years old. You may find grandmothers and grandfathers playing at their local playing field. Getting hit by a paintball may hurt a little bit at first but you will get used to it. People who play regularly say that it is more the shock than the pain you feel.

But there are also experts who say that paintball is a game, which makes people aggressive because you shoot at people even if they don't get hurt. In their opinion it is a bit like playing an ego shooter in real life. Some psychologists think that paintball players might get too interested in war and weapons. They might lose the feeling that it is not okay to shoot another human being.

1. Tick (✓) the correct answer

1. Paintball is

A		no sport.
B		getting more and more popular.
C		very dangerous.
D		only for very athletic people.

2. For playing paintball you must

A		spend a lot of money.
B		be an adult.
C		have team spirit.
D		be young and fit.

3. Some people say that

A		paintball is good against stress.
B		playing paintball is very painful.
C		everybody should play paintball.
D		paintball is an expensive sport.

4. Critics think that

A		paintball does not make people aggressive.
B		playing paintball might be dangerous.
C		paintball is too much about shooting people.
D		you feel too much pain.

2. Answer the following questions

1. When and where was paintball invented?
2. What is the aim of the game?
3. What does the equipment consist of?

III WRITING TASK

Look at the pictures and write a story of about 180 words.

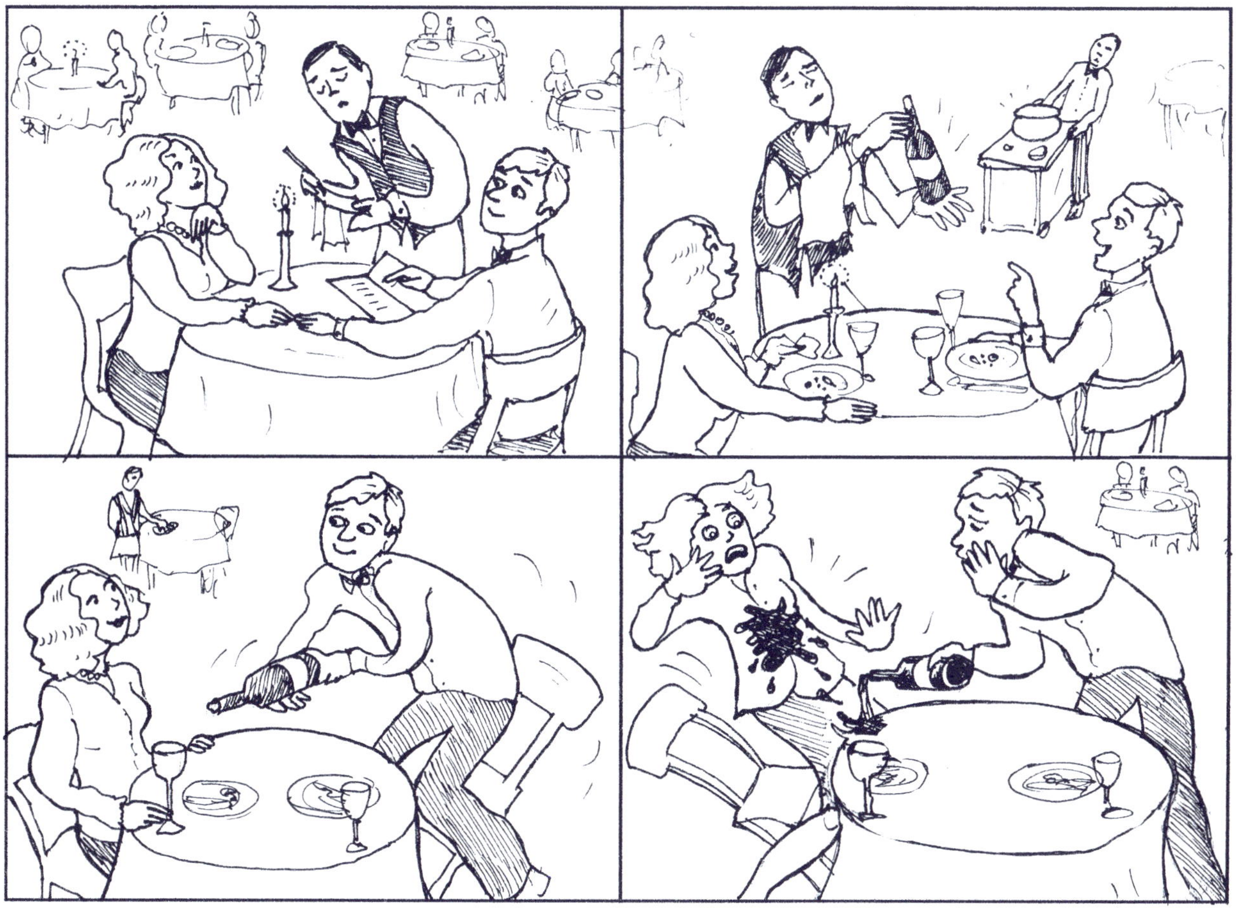

TEST 6

I FOCUS ON GRAMMAR

1. Fill in the suitable phrasal verbs: (look for, hold on, watch out, put up with, look after, check in)

1. I don't want to ______________________ his bad behaviour any longer.
2. Excuse me, I'm ______________________ Mr. Brown. Do you know where he is?
3. Can I talk to your boss? - ______________________ , I'll try to find her.
4. As soon as you ______________________ at the reception you will get a key.
5. ______________________ , this is a dangerous crossing!
6. I can't come with you. I've got to ______________________ my little brother.

2. Use an adverb of degree in box A and an adjective/adverb in box B to make six meaningful English sentences!

A	B
extremely, really, nearly, hardly, rather, fairly, totally, terribly	*interesting, slowly, dark, small, bad, good, dangerous, boring, tired, stupid, funny, exciting*

3. Fill in adjective or adverb

1. You need not see the film. It's ______________________ (real) terrible.
2. Sandra understands Italian ______________________ (perfect).
3. "The Secret Life of Bees" is such an ______________________ (interesting) book.
I couldn't stop reading.
4. Ann looks ______________________ (awful) in this dress.
She should never wear ______________________ (short) dresses.
5. Mrs Brown has not been at work for four days now.
I hope she is not ______________________ (serious) ill.
6. Let's meet at the pub in the evening! –Yeah, sounds ______________________ (great).

II READING COMPREHENSION

Being a vegetarian

There are various reasons why people are vegetarians. Some have taken this step because of their religion, others because they are worried about the way animals are treated in farming. Other people think that a vegetarian lifestyle is healthier. For many vegetarians it is a mixture of reasons that made them decide to stop eating meat. One woman says, "I grew up on a farm and I never liked the idea of killing and eating my animal friends."

It seems that vegetarianism is becoming more and more popular, especially among younger people. There are studies that show that a vegetarian diet can be good for your health because it can reduce the risk of heart diseases and some cancers. But it is very important to get enough proteins.

The reasons for becoming a vegetarian are different for each person. Sally Miller says that eating meat made her feel tired. "That's the main reason why I stopped eating meat. I feel so much better now and have a lot more energy." Other people think of the poor people in the world. Most of the livestock (Vieh) that is eaten by humans is grain (Getreide) fed. The grain we feed the animals could be made into food for many humans all over the world.

Sometimes being a vegetarian can be difficult, especially when the people around you cannot understand your decision and want to convince you that you can't lead a happy life without eating meat. Some people may look at you a bit curiously. Being the only vegetarian in your family can also be a problem, e.g. if your family want to go to a fast food restaurant.

Some people are semi-vegetarians. They eat mainly vegetarian food but also fish, sometimes even poultry (Geflügel) and dairy products and eggs.

A radical form of vegetarianism is the vegan lifestyle. It means not eating or using any animal products. A vegan doesn't eat meat, eggs, dairy products, or honey and avoids wearing leather and using products tested on animals. Vegans eat grain, nuts, fruits and vegetables.

Mark the following statements true (T) or false (F)

	T	F
1. Most people are vegetarians because of religious reasons.		
2. Eating vegetarian food may be good for your heart.		
3. Some vegetarians feel tired because they do not eat meat.		
4. It is quite easy to live as a vegetarian.		
5. All vegetarians eat fish.		
6. Vegans don't eat any animal products.		
7. Most people become vegetarians for the same reason.		

III WRITING TASK

Write a text about a visit to a restaurant you enjoyed/didn't enjoy very much.

Think about:

- choice of food (Did they have what you liked?)
- service (Were the waiters/waitresses friendly?)
- the atmosphere (Was it nice/over the top/dirty?)
- the people who were with you (Did they have a good/bad time?)
- problems (Did anything go wrong?)

Your text should be about 150–180 words.

TEST 7

I FOCUS ON GRAMMAR

1. Fill in the correct form of the verb

1. If you took a taxi you ______________________ (catch) the train.
2. I'm sure Tom would take you around Vienna if you ______________________ (ask) him.
3. What ______________________ (you, do) if you got lost in New York?
4. I usually ______________________ (go) by underground if I am not in a hurry.
5. If you had enough money you ______________________ (can do) your shopping on Fifth Avenue.
6. Someone ______________________ (steal) your bike if you leave it unlocked.

2. Circle the correct word or phrase

1. My mum finally gave up to smoke/smoking when she was forty.
2. I really enjoy watching/to watch MTV. Some of the music videos are really great.
3. My English pen friend told me he is looking forward to see/seeing me.
4. I'd really like visiting/to visit New York one day. I have heard so much about it already.
5. Don't let the cat sleeping/sleep in your bed!
6. Stop to chat/chatting with your neighbour! This is a difficult grammar chapter.
7. You should practise speaking/to speak English every day to improve your pronunciation.
8. As the weather was wonderful my dad suggested having/to have picnic down by the river.
9. Time seems to pass/passing more quickly when you are having fun.
10. When I was ten I was afraid to fly/of flying.

3. Choose the correct answer

1. I asked my little sister if ______________________ finished her homework.

a. she would　　c. she was
b. she had　　d. she had been

2. Tina apologised ______________________ juice stains on my new jeans.

a. that she got　　c. to get
b. for getting　　d. for she gets

3. George promised ______________________ me paint my room at the weekend.

a. helping　　c. that he helps
b. to help　　d. for helping

4. Mum suggested ______________________ to Ireland in the summer holidays.

a. to go　　c. going
b. for going　　d. that we went

4. Complete the sentences (reported speech)

1. "I'm meeting my aunt Jenny tomorrow," Carla said.

Carla said she ____________________ her aunt Jenny ____________________.

2. "My mum gave me twenty Euros yesterday," Nathan said.

Nathan said his mum ____________________ twenty Euros ____________________.

3. "I've lost my wallet at the shopping mall," Fred complained.

Fred complained that he ___________________________ at the shopping mall.

4. "I'm sure I'll sleep like a baby tonight," Anne remarked.

Anne remarked that she ____________________ that she ____________________ like a baby ____________________.

5. "Have you been to the fashion show?" Maria asked.

Maria asked _________ I ____________________ to the fashion show.

II USE OF ENGLISH

1. Find the British equivalents for the following American words

1. French fries ____________________
2. apartment ____________________
3. vacation ____________________
4. elevator ____________________
5. fall ____________________
6. purse ____________________
7. movie ____________________
8. sidewalk ____________________
9. pants ____________________
10. restroom ____________________

2. One of the words in each sentence is in the wrong form. Write the correct word

1. There are people who believe that some parts of New York are not save. _____________
2. In big cities it is quite danger to ride your bike without wearing a helmet. _____________
3. Scientists worry about the destroying of the environment. ________________________
4. Air pollute is a serious problem, especially in megacities. ________________________
5. The nature environment of a wild animal is called "habitat". ________________________
6. Skateboard must be an interesting hobby. _________________________________
7. I am very interesting in environmental problems. _______________________________

III READING COMPREHENSION

Air Pollution and Global Warming

Every day, the average person breathes in about 20,000 litres of air. Every time we breathe, we risk inhaling dangerous chemicals that have found their way into the air.

Air pollution can have serious consequences for the health of human beings, and it also affects the environment. Because it is located in the atmosphere, air pollution is able to travel easily. Though some pollution comes from natural sources, such as forest fires and volcanic eruptions, most pollution is the result of human activity. Fossil fuel-burning power plants and automobiles are responsible for about 90% of all air pollution in the United States. Places like Mexico City and Sao Paulo have some of the most dangerous pollution levels in the world.

Global warming is also known as the greenhouse effect. The greenhouse effect is warming the planet and threatening the environment. What scares people is the fact that global warming is happening at such a rapid pace. Some scientists predict that over the next century, the global temperature will rise by several degrees.

One of the largest factors contributing to global warming is the problem of overpopulation and its many effects. The growing number of people need more items which take more energy to make. They also drive more cars, and create larger amounts of garbage. These factors all increase the global warming problem.

What the effects of global warming will be in the future is extremely difficult to say. Scientists use computer models to study the effects of global warming. Some scientists say global warming has already been going on for a while. Others say that we do not have enough information now to know for sure.

Most scientists are convinced that greenhouse gases are warming the Earth. What they are still trying to figure out is how quickly temperatures are rising, and what will happen as a result. The climate changes that will result from global warming are extremely difficult to predict. The rise in sea levels, for example, would be a big problem for some places. Islands would disappear, and coastlines all over the world would be flooded. Global warming could cause a major catastrophe.

1. Tick (✓) the correct answer(s)

1. Air pollution

A		affects people's health.
B		affects the environment.
C		has no effects.

2. Most pollution

A		comes from natural sources.
B		is the result of human activity.
C		is caused by global warming.

3. In the future global temperatures

A		will rise.
B		will fall.
C		will probably stay the same.

4. The effects of global warming

A		are easy to predict.
B		are difficult to predict.
C		can easily be controlled.

2. Mark the following statements true (T) or false (F)

	T	F
1. Every day we breathe in about 25,000 litres of air.		
2. Air pollution can travel easily.		
3. Global warming is also known as the glasshouse affect.		

4. The most dangerous levels of pollution can be found in Mexico City and Los Angeles.		
5. Overpopulation and its effects contribute to global warming.		
6. The rise in sea levels would flood coastlines all over the world.		

IV WRITING TASK

Liz is a flight attendant. In a short text she explains what she has to do as a flight attendant and what she likes/dislikes about her job.

Make sure your text includes:

- working hours
- duties (Aufgaben, Pflichten)
- income
- possible problems (e.g. difficult passengers, lot of travelling ...)

Your text should be about 120–150 words.

TEST 8

I FOCUS ON GRAMMAR

1. If the verb in bold (fettgedruckt) is correct, put a tick (✓). If it is wrong, write the correct form of the verb.

1. I hope I'll be able **to drive** as soon as I am seventeen.

____

2. My mum suggested **to paint** my room blue but I hate blue.

____

3. I'd really like **visiting** London one day. I have heard so much about it.

____

4. Stop **to write** and hand in the test papers.

____

5. Don't let the dog **sleeping** on the bed.

____

6. Where is my English book? I remember **putting** it on my desk.

____

7. My mum has decided **looking** for a job again.

____

8. I can't imagine **to have** to live without a computer or a TV set.

____

9. The children enjoyed **reading** their first real English book.

____

10. On the way to the ski camp we stopped **to have** lunch at a fast food restaurant.

____

2. Put the following sentences into reported speech

1. "May I use my English dictionary?" Charly wanted to know.
2. "Don't drop the glass!" my mum told my little sister.
3. Joan said, "I'll visit Ben if he decides to go to London for a year."
4. "I found an old Roman coin in the garden yesterday," he told us.
5. "Will you be here for the next ten minutes?" she asked him.
6. "I can't go swimming because I have to finish my homework first," John said.

3. Use the -ing form of the verb or the infinitive

1. Linda wants to become a flight attendant because she enjoys ____________________ (go) to foreign countries.
2. Could you please stop ____________________ (make) so much noise?

I can't concentrate on my work.

3. There was a lot of traffic but we managed ________________ (get) to the airport in time.
4. Peter is interested in ________________ (learn) English. He needs it for his future job.
5. She promised ________________ (come) earlier and help us.

4. Complete the sentences using the correct form of the verb in brackets

1. If I ________________ (get) a good mark in my next English test, my parents will buy me a new mobile phone.
2. If my brother borrowed my CDs without asking, I ________________ (scream).
3. Susan will be very upset if Peter ________________ (not come) to her birthday party.
4. If I were you, I ________________ (eat) less chocolate. You need to lose weight.
5. If she ________________ (not live) in the country, she would go out more often.
6. It would be very bad for our health if we only ________________ (eat) chocolate and crisps.

5. Circle the correct word or phrase

1. If Ann paid more attention in class, she **will/would** learn more.
2. You wouldn't put on so much weight if you **don't/didn't** eat so much fast food.
3. If **I live/lived** closer to the school, I could ride my bike to school.
4. If I **am/were** you, I would tell my parents the truth.
5. **Will/would** Linda be upset if I didn't invite her to my birthday party?
6. My mum says that if I stop eating meat, my body **didn't/won't** get all the things it needs to stay healthy.

II USE OF ENGLISH

1. Choose the correct answer

1. What ________________ when the earthquake hit?

a) have you done b) were you doing c) are you doing d) do you do

2. Leonardo da Vinci, ________ was also a famous inventor, painted the famous Mona Lisa.

a) which b) that c) who d) what

3. I hope we're going to stay ________ some nice B&Bs when we are in Wales this summer.

a) to b) with c) on d) at

4. Michaela knows New York quite well because she ________________ there.

a) used live b) used to living c) was used to live d) used to live

5. Oh no! My bike ________________ ! I forgot to lock it!

a) was stealing b) stole c) has been stolen d) was being stolen

6. I am tired because I ________________ English all afternoon.

a) have studied b) studied c) have been studying d) had studied

7. I am really thirsty. Do you think I could have ________________ water, please?

a) some b) any c) few d) much

8. If there is a word you don't know the meaning of, look it ________________ in a dictionary.

a) for b) at c) up d) after

III READING COMPREHENSION

1.Choose the sentence (a, b or c) which means the same as the first sentence

1. I have to do some work on my project today.
a) I've already finished the project.
b) I need to work on the project.
c) I haven't got time to work on my project.

2. Leon didn't have to go to the headmaster's office.
a) It was not necessary for Leon to go to the headmaster's office.
b) Leon went to the headmaster's office.
c) Leon is going to see the headmaster.

3. Students must not use their mobile phones during lessons.
a) Students can use their mobile phones if they want to.
b) Using your mobile phone during lessons is not allowed.
c) Students don't use mobile phones during lessons.

4. In case of a fire alarm all students must leave the school building.
a) In case of a fire alarm students can leave the school building.
b) In case of a fire alarm students need to leave the school building.
c) In case of a fire alarm students should stay in the school building.

5. We have to learn the poem by heart.
a) We need to learn the poem by heart.
b) We may learn the poem by heart.
c) We can learn the poem by heart.

6. Smoking is not allowed in the school yard.
a) You can smoke in the school yard.
b) Smoking is forbidden in the school yard.
c) Students don't smoke in the school yard.

7. The instructions tell you to write in pencil.
a) You can write in pencil.
b) You must write in pencil.
c) You are allowed to write in pencil.

8. If you want to pass the exam, you must do some revision.
a) You mustn't do any revision if you want to pass the exam.
b) You can do some revision if you want to pass the exam.
c) It is necessary to do some revision if you want to pass the exam.

IV WRITING TASK

Write a (short) story

Use one of the following texts as the beginning of your story.

1. For Kay Donovan reading was life. Her idea of heaven was an afternoon with a good book and a bag of crisps. One day when she was reading her favourite book something really strange happened.
2. I looked around the room. Nothing seemed unusual, but then ...
3. When Bob Sanders woke up on Monday morning, he found he was a girl. He was standing, staring at himself in the mirror, when his mother came in.
4. This was not home! The grass was orange and in the sky we saw ...
5. It was getting dark and we were scared. We had no idea where we were. Why had we not stayed close to the campsite?

Your story should be about 150 words.

TEST 9

I FOCUS ON GRAMMAR

1. Fill in who/which/that where necessary

1. An old woman, ____________ was carrying a shopping bag, got on the bus.
2. Did you see Molly at the weekend? – No, Friday after school was the last time ____________ I saw her.
3. Do you know ____________ this new horror book was written by?
4. Yesterday Sue went to this new Indian restaurant. The dish __________ she tried was very spicy.
5. The train ____________ leaves from platform two goes to Hamburg.
6. When we were in Australia we got lost once because we took a road ____________ ended in the middle of nowhere.
7. Here is a picture of the hotel ____________ we stayed at in Rome last year.
8. Are all the students ____________ take part in the exchange programme here?
9. Is this the CD ____________ you ordered?
10. I started talking to some boys ____________ were waiting at the bus stop.

2. Circle the extra word in each sentence you don't need

1. The girl who she lives next door is called Sarah.
2. Peter, whose his brother is a policeman, wants to be an engineer.
3. The car, which my father bought it last week, is red.
4. The Millers, who they got married last year, have sold their house.

3. Complete each second sentence so that it has a similar (gleiche) meaning to the first sentence

1. It was not hot, so we were not thirsty.
If it ______________________________ hot, we would have been thirsty.
2. Sally didn't have tickets, so we didn't go to the concert.
If Sally ______________________________ tickets, we'd have gone to the concert.
3. They left the cinema because the film was so boring.
They ______________________________ the cinema if the film hadn't been so boring.
4. I didn't buy any books because I found nothing interesting.
I ______________________________ some books if I had found something interesting.

II READING COMPREHENSION

A job for everyone?

You don't have to be beautiful to work in the film business. Even if you're overweight, underweight, short, got no teeth, are bald or over 70 years old – some film company may be looking just for you.

In any TV drama, comedy series, or commercial you'll see a lot of very normal looking people in the background. Filmmakers and advertising agencies want street scenes to look real. They don't need people who look like George Clooney or Keira Knightley. What they want is people who look like the average person.

Some people do this kind of job full time. It's a question of being with the right agency and of living in the right area.

Bill, who is over 50, has got half his teeth and is bald, but he got four days work in a forthcoming TV Comedy series. He had to be at the set early in the morning, at 7 am and he was still there at 6 pm, but in that time he was given three good meals and actually worked for about 2 hours a day. The rest of the time he spent sitting on a Crew Coach reading, listening to music, doing sudokus, or chatting with other people.

Bill got £ 56 for a day's work. This is not very much, but once you've done one such job, a casting executive might see your face on the screen or in the agency portfolio and you might be asked to do more work. If this happens, you might earn more money. Sometimes a director may ask for one particular person he wants to see more in the foreground because he/she suits the part. Those people might be paid as much as £ 200 per day.

Maybe you are just the person people in the film business are looking for. So send a photo and short CV (curriculum vitae) to some casting and model agencies. You might be lucky. Of course, you are not going to be a big star or to become rich. But you may find an interesting way to earn some extra money.

Mark the following statements true (T) or false (F)

	T	F
1. Only beautiful people appear in films.		
2. George Clooney looks like an average person.		
3. Bill does this job full time.		
4. Bill only worked for two hours a day.		
5. Sometimes the film people ask for one particular person.		
6. Bill was not given anything to eat all day.		
7. It's a good idea to send your photo to a casting agency.		

III WRITING TASK

Over the centuries people have invented the strangest things.

Choose one of the two inventions and write its history.

Be sure to mention:

- who invented it
- why it was invented
- how it works
- how it makes life easier for people
- what problems there might be ...

Your text should be 180–200 words.

a) The "dishwasher-emptier"

b) The "finding-lost-things-machine"

TEST 10

I FOCUS ON GRAMMAR

1. Choose the sentence (a or b) which means the same as the first sentence

1. She'd left when her boyfriend arrived.
a) Her boyfriend arrived and then she left.
b) She left and then her boyfriend arrived.

2. By the time Mary decided to help me I had cleaned the kitchen.
a) I cleaned the kitchen before Mary decided to help me.
b) I cleaned the kitchen after Mary decided to help me.

3. Peter didn't fall asleep before his mum had read him a bedtime story.
a) Peter fell asleep and then his mum read him a bedtime story.
b) His mum read him a bedtime story and then Peter fell asleep.

4. We had ordered the tickets before we heard about the cheaper offer.
a) We ordered the tickets and then we heard about the cheaper offer.
b) We heard about the cheaper offer and then we ordered the tickets. ✓

2. Fill in the correct forms of past simple, past progressive, present perfect simple, present perfect progressive or past perfect

1. Yesterday I met (meet) Paul who ______ (be) my best friend in kindergarten.
2. Have you ever seen (you/ever/see) such an ugly dog? ✓
3. I was had reading (read) a thrilling book when my brother called (call) to tell me that our uncle had had had (have) an accident.
4. I'd like to go to Russia this summer. I have never been (never/be) there before. ✓ Sam says it is very interesting. He was (be) there last year. ✓
5. After Andrew had left (leave) his wife he had (have) a lot of problems. ✓
6. While I was looking (look) for a parking space my friend waited was waiting (wait) for me in front of the cinema.
7. I think John must have forgotten the meeting. We had waited (wait) for an hour now and he is still not here. have been waiting

3. Conditionals: Complete the sentences using the correct form of the verb

1. If Sally ______ (pass) the exam, her grandpa will buy her a new iPod.
2. He wouldn't mind if we ______ (stop) at his place.
3. If you don't eat the cake, granny ______ (be) upset.

4. I would have been there on time if I ___________________________ (not miss) the bus.
5. If I were you, I ___________________________ (buy) the red sweater.

II READING COMPREHENSION

The story of St. Patrick

St. Patrick, the patron saint of Ireland, lived at the end of the 4th and the beginning of the 5th century. He was born in Wales. When he was fourteen years old he was taken to Ireland as a slave. For six years he had to work very hard on a farm. He often prayed to God and one night God told him that he had to escape. Patrick managed to get to a port where he asked the captain of a ship transporting wolfhounds to France to take him on board. The captain didn't want to have a slave on his ship and sent Patrick away. But when the ship was about to leave the pier the hounds began to bark and to behave like mad. So the ship had to return. When they tried again later the same thing happened. Now Patrick saw his chance. He told the captain that he would calm the dogs if the captain took him to France. The captain agreed and really, when Patrick boarded the ship the hounds became quiet. So Patrick got to France and from there back to his family in Wales.

Soon Patrick found out that he wanted to become a priest. Later he returned to Ireland to become a missionary. It was Easter when he arrived in Ireland. Patrick and the other priests, who had come with him, decided that they wanted to light a fire. That night was also a very special night for the Irish people who were no Christians. They were celebrating the coming of spring. Usually their king lit a fire as a sign for all the other people to light their fires. But now Patrick had lit his fire first. The Irish king was very angry and sent people to put out Patrick's fire but they couldn't. Only Patrick could do it.

Soon Patrick began to talk to the people. They were surprised that he could speak their language so well. He told them about the Christian God and about Jesus. So he brought Christianity to Ireland.

A legend says that Patrick drove the snakes from Ireland. He was standing on a hill and with a wooden stick drove the snakes into the sea. There are really no snakes in Ireland but this may be because Ireland is an island separated from the continent, so the snakes could not get there. Besides, snakes were a common symbol in many old Irish religions. The story of St. Patrick and the snakes is a symbol of Christianity replacing pagan (heidnisch) religions in Ireland.

Each year on March 17th the Irish all over the world celebrate St. Patrick's Day.

Tick (✓) the correct answer

1. St. Patrick was

A		English.
B	✓	Irish.
C		Welsh.
D		French.

2. Patrick worked for a

A		farmer.
B		priest.
C		slave.
D		king.

3. The captain did not want Patrick on his ship because

A		it was full of dogs.
B		the dogs were too loud.
C		he didn't like Irish people.
D		Patrick was a slave.

4. Patrick came back to Ireland

A		on St. Patrick's Day.
B		at Easter.
C		because he was homesick.
D		to learn the language.

5. St. Patrick

A		brought Christianity to Ireland.
B		brought snakes to Ireland.
C		brought wolfhounds to Ireland.
D		brought the pagan religion to Ireland.

6. Snakes were a symbol of

A		Christianity.
B		the Irish king.
C		many pagan religions.
D		Ireland.

III WRITING TASK

Imagine your mother or father has been offered a super job in Spain/England/India/USA (choose one country). Your parents have just told you that they have decided to accept the offer. That means that you will be moving to this country.

Write an e-mail to your best friend telling him/her the news.
Write about your feelings, your hopes, your fears ...

Your text should be 150–180 words.

Aufsteigen in ...

Berger, Astrid; Broniowski, Gabriele
Aufsteigen in Englisch 4
So schaffst du die 4. Klasse HS/AHS/NMS
(mit Lösungsheft)

Kt., 76 Seiten, Format 21 x 29,7 cm
978-3-7074-0761-7

Reisch, Renate
Aufsteigen Business Englisch 1
So schaffst du die 2. Klasse HASCH/3. Klasse HAK
(mit Lösungsheft)

Kt., 56 Seiten, Format 21 x 29,7 cm
978-3-7074-1150-8

www.ggverlag.at

Schulbuchnummer 155365

1. Auflage 2010, Nachdruck 2013 (1,02)

Umschlagillustration: Elena Obermüller
Innenillustrationen: Natasha Chalmers
Printed by Brüder Glöckler, Wöllersdorf

ISBN 978-3-7074-1198-0

Aufsteigen ... Englisch 4 Schularbeiten

LÖSUNGSHEFT

G&G

4

1. If I **get** a good mark in my next English test, my parents will buy me a new mobile phone.
2. If my brother borrowed my CDs without asking, I **would scream.**
3. Susan will be very upset if Peter **does not come** to her birthday party.
4. If I were you, I **would eat** less chocolate. You need to lose weight.
5. If she **did not live** in the country, she would go out more often.
6. It would be very bad for our health if we only **ate** chocolate and crisps.

5

1. If Ann paid more attention in class, she **would** learn more.
2. You wouldn't put on so much weight if you **didn't** eat so much fast food.
3. If I **lived** closer to the school, I could ride my bike to school.
4. If I **were** you, I would tell my parents the truth.
5. **Would** Linda be upset if I didn't invite her to my birthday party?
6. My mum says that if I stop eating meat, my body **won't** get all the things it needs to stay healthy.

II USE OF ENGLISH

1B, 2C, 3D, 4D, 5C, 6C, 7A, 8C

III READING COMPREHENSION

1B, 2A, 3B, 4B, 5A, 6B, 7B, 8C

TEST 9

I FOCUS ON GRAMMAR

1

1. An old woman, **who** was carrying a shopping bag, got on the bus.
2. Did you see Molly at the weekend? – No, Friday after school was the last time I saw her.
3. Do you know **who** this new horror book was written by?
4. Yesterday Sue went to this new Indian restaurant. The dish she tried was very spicy.
5. The train **which/that** leaves from platform two goes to Hamburg.
6. When we were in Australia we got lost once because we took a road **which/that** ended in the middle of nowhere.
7. Here is a picture of the hotel we stayed at in Rome last year.
8. Are all the students **who** take part in the exchange programme here?
9. Is this the CD you ordered?
10. I started talking to some boys **who** were waiting at the bus stop.

2

1. The girl who lives next door is called Sarah.
2. Peter, whose brother is a policeman, wants to be an engineer.
3. The car, which my father bought last week, is red.
4. The Millers, who got married last year, have sold their house.

3

1. If it **had been** hot, we would have been thirsty.
2. If Sally **had had** tickets, we'd have gone to the concert.
3. They **would not have left** the cinema if the film hadn't been so boring.
4. I **would have bought** some books if I had found something interesting.

II READING COMPREHENSION

1F, 2F, 3F, 4T, 5T, 6F, 7T

TEST 10

I FOCUS ON GRAMMAR

1

1B, 2A, 3B, 4A

2

1. Yesterday I **met** Paul who **had been** my best friend in kindergarten.
2. **Have you ever seen** such an ugly dog?
3. I **was reading** a thrilling book when my brother **called** to tell me that our uncle **h** an accident.
4. I'd like to go to Russia this summer. I **have never been** there before. Sam says it is very interesting. He **was** there last year.
5. After Andrew **had left** his wife he **had** a lot of problems.
6. While I **was looking** for a parking space my friend **was waiting** for me in front
7. I think John must have forgotten the meeting. We **have been waiting** for an hou he is still not here.

3

1. If Sally **passes** the exam, her grandpa will buy her a new iPod.
2. He wouldn't mind if we **stopped** at his place.
3. If you don't eat the cake, granny **will be** upset.
4. I would have been there on time if I **had not missed** the bus.
5. If I were you, I **would buy** the red sweater.

II READING COMPREHENSION

1C, 2A, 3D, 4B, 5A, 6C